Thriving as an International Student in the UK

Thriving as an International Student in the UK

Your Comprehensive Guide to Success and Well-being

Patience Bamisaye

Copyright © 2024 by Patience Bamisaye

All rights reserved. No part of this book may be reproduced or used in any manner without written permission of the copyright owner except for the use of quotations in a book review.

FIRST EDITION

ISBNs:
Paperback: 978-1-80541-323-3
Hardback: 978-1-80541-325-7
eBook: 978-1-80541-324-0

International students from various countries choose to pursue their higher education in the UK as the standard is very high and respected all over the world. The transition from home to any host country for higher education may be an exciting experience, but some students may find it challenging due to various reasons. There are no universally appropriate or inappropriate coping strategies. Some coping strategies may work effectively in some situations but may not be suitable for others. People may use active (positive) coping strategies, such as planning, seeking social support for instrumental and emotional reasons, and making positive reinterpretation and acceptance. On the other hand, people may use avoidant (negative) coping strategies, including aggression, passive aggression, and suppression of their problems.

Based on personal experience, international students face different challenges. They include culture shifts, language problems, lack of support, perceived discrimination, low self-efficacy, poor interaction with others, academic problems, loneliness, cultural stress, financial problems, unsuitable food, different weather, family problems, psychological problems and other factors.

This book addresses some of the issues international students struggle with while in the UK for their course of study. It aims to increase awareness of potential sources of problems for international students and offers some coping strategies. Thereby, it facilitates better preparedness for students as well as a better understanding for universities to support them.

The author is an alumnus of one of the universities in England and bases her lived experience around her time at that university.

CHAPTER ONE
Author's Personal Experience

As an alumni member and a senior lecturer of International and Adult Nursing in the Faculty of Health, Education, Medicine and Social Care, I acknowledge that my university experience contributed to my success and helped shape me into who I am today.

I arrived in the United Kingdom (UK) for the first time in September 2011, after I realised that as a registered nurse/midwife in my country (I had a Diploma in Nursing), I needed to take my career to the next level. I was nervous about travelling outside of my home country for the first time, and I did not have any family or friends in the UK. However, the student admission process at my university had a great strategy for welcoming international students. They provided free pickup from the airport and made arrangements for me to book my accommodation on campus before even stepping foot

Author's Personal Experience

in the UK. This part of my experience was very special and is worth emulating by those universities that admit international students. It is very reassuring to come to a place for the first time and not have to worry about transportation from the airport or accommodation.

If I am asked to describe the day I landed in the UK for the first time, I say freezing! Everybody said it was warm, as it was, of course, summer in the UK, but I was coming from West Africa, with much higher temperatures. I remember that even the cardigan I put on could not provide me with the kind of warmth I needed. The temperature then was said to be about 12 degrees, yet people around me were saying it was warm. That was a shock to me! For someone coming from over 30 degrees, you can imagine that 12 degrees would, indeed, be freezing for them.

Patience Bamisaye

Meet and greet

Right from the first point of arrival at Heathrow Airport, I began making friends with the buddies from my university who came along to meet the new students. Again, this was very helpful as it was reassuring and made me feel less anxious straight away. Another favourable thing was the fact that the student buddies sent to the airport from the university were people of the same nationality as me. This made it even easier to start a conversation and share experiences. An international student is more likely to feel relaxed and at home when approached by someone who has a lot in common with them.

You cannot imagine the amount of fear, anxiety and uncertainties the international students enter the country with, having left all of their families and loved ones thousands of miles away and finding themselves in a completely different environment. From my personal experience, these student buddies deliver outstanding support and opportunities for students. They are passionate about promoting student engagement, which had a hugely positive effect on my student experience at the university.

During my first week as a student, I was extremely fortunate to attend a comprehensive and informative induction session, which provided me with a wealth of information about the support and resources available to students on campus. I was amazed by the variety of services available, including academic support, mental health counselling, career guidance, and much more. The session was so well-structured and thorough that I left with a clear understanding of how to access these resources whenever I needed them.

This knowledge gave me tremendous peace of mind and security, knowing that I had access to a wide range of support services to help me navigate the challenges of student life. Even when I felt homesick and overwhelmed by the new environment, I knew that I could turn to the counselling services for guidance and support. The counsellors were kind, empathetic and understanding, and they provided me with the tools and resources I needed to cope with my challenges. Thanks to the comprehensive induction session and the support services available, I had an extremely positive and fulfilling experience during my time as a student.

As an individual who has studied abroad, I cannot stress enough the importance of attending orientation sessions as an international student. These sessions are an invaluable opportunity to learn about the university's culture, policies and expectations, and to meet other international students who share similar challenges and experiences. Universities that organise orientation sessions and international days demonstrate a strong commitment to supporting their international student community and creating a welcoming environment.

In my personal experience, my university went above and beyond to support international students in fulfilling their academic and personal goals. They provided a range of resources, such as academic advising, language support, and cultural programming, that helped me navigate the unfamiliar terrain of studying abroad. Furthermore, the university's commitment to providing students with hands-on experiences and practical skills has been instrumental in preparing me for my future career. Therefore, attending orientation sessions and taking advantage of the resources offered by universities is crucial for international students to thrive and succeed academically and personally. I encourage universities to continue their efforts to support their international student community and provide them with the tools and experiences they need to achieve their full potential.

During my time at university, I was actively engaged in various extracurricular activities that helped me grow as a person. One such activity was volunteering as a student ambassador and buddy to support other students, just like I was helped on my first day. Being aware of all the support and opportunities I received in my life, I felt a sense of gratitude and humbleness that made me want to give back to the community.

I was passionate about supporting others through the ups and downs of life, and this drove me to become the course representative for the BSc International Nursing Studies students. As a course rep, I went above and beyond to provide exceptional support to my coursemates, without exception. I helped them with their coursework, answered their queries, and provided emotional support when needed.

Author's Personal Experience

My hard work and dedication were recognised when I was awarded the Best Student Rep of the Year on my campus in 2012. This was one of my proudest moments at the university, and it showed me that exceptional work is always rewarded at UK universities like mine. I am grateful for this experience that taught me the value of giving back to the community and helping others in need.

After earning my bachelor's degree, I decided to go back to my home country to spend some time with my family. However, I realised that I wanted to pursue a career in nursing in the UK. So, in 2015, I returned to the UK to complete my Master's in Nursing as part of the Overseas Nurse Programme (ONP).

The ONP is a programme approved by the Nursing & Midwifery Council (NMC) that assesses your ability to practise in the UK healthcare environment. The programme consists of a few weeks of protected learning time and, where appropriate, a period of supervised placement practice. The NMC will send you a decision letter that confirms what parts of the programme you need to undertake. If you have already had educational and practical experience in your home country that closely matches UK requirements for entry to the register, you may only need to take about four weeks of protected learning period. However, if you don't have the required educational and practical experience, you may need to take additional courses and placement practices to gain the necessary skills and knowledge.

Furthermore, you need to pass the International English Language Testing System (IELTS) exams, which are mandatory for all overseas nurses. I successfully passed the IELTS exams, which made me eligible for registration to practise as a nurse in the UK.

Author's Personal Experience

It is important to note that this is an old process of getting a nursing registration in the UK; the Nursing and Midwifery Council (NMC) has now replaced this process with Computer-Based Test (CBT) and Objective Structured Clinical Exams (OSCE). These exams are more rigorous and comprehensive and test your ability to communicate effectively, make sound clinical decisions, and provide safe and effective care to patients.

During my professional career, I had the opportunity to work in the National Health Service (NHS) for several years. This experience enabled me to gain extensive knowledge and expertise in all areas of nursing care, both in hospitals and communities. It was an enriching experience that helped me grow and develop my skills as a nurse. After this, I decided to move into clinical practice with one of the NHS Trusts, where I worked as part of the upper and lower gastrointestinal surgery team. This was an exciting and challenging role, which allowed me to develop my clinical skills further, particularly in the field of surgery.

My experience as an international nurse working in the NHS was like a roller coaster journey. I had my fair share of ups and downs, but overall, it was an incredibly rewarding experience. As with any career, there were times when I faced difficulties and challenges. However, I always tried to stay positive and focused on my goals. Despite the challenges, I was able to achieve my goals and progress in my career. The journey was not always easy, and there were times when I felt like giving up, but I always reminded myself of why I started and what I wanted to achieve. Looking back, I can say that working in the NHS was a life-changing experience. It provided me with valuable skills and knowledge that I still use today. It was not always easy, but

Author's Personal Experience

I have learned to appreciate the good, bad, and ugly moments that I experienced while working with the NHS. These experiences have inspired me to share my story with others and write a book about my journey as an overseas nurse working in the UK.

The process of adjusting to a new work environment can be challenging for international nurses and healthcare workers, as they may need to adapt to a new culture, language, and healthcare system. To ensure that they can assimilate into the new environment and maximise their training, it is vital to have proper planning, preparation, and support from clinical facilitators. Without such support, international healthcare providers may struggle to work independently in the NHS.

As someone who has worked as an overseas nurse in the NHS, I understand the challenges faced by international nurses and healthcare workers. This experience has stimulated my professional curiosity to investigate the lived experience of international nurses in the UK, with a particular focus on culture shock. As part of my doctorate programme, I plan to undertake a research project that explores this topic in greater detail, and I hope to share the outcome in my next book.

Through this study, I aim to uncover the specific needs of overseas nurses during their induction process before they start working in the NHS. By doing so, I hope to highlight the need for greater support and assistance for international nurses and healthcare workers to ensure that they can provide the best possible care to patients in the UK.

As someone who spent a few years working in the NHS, I consider myself fortunate to have landed my dream job as a clinical skills tutor at a prestigious university in the UK. In this role,

Author's Personal Experience

I had the opportunity to train adult nursing students and develop my career prospects even further. From my experience, I can confidently say that international students who come to the UK to study have an excellent chance of securing employment in their desired field if they are willing to work hard and pursue their goals. The UK offers a plethora of job opportunities across various industries, and with the right qualifications and skills, students can make a successful transition from being a student to becoming a professional. I believe that the UK education system provides a great foundation for students to launch their careers. With dedication and perseverance, they can achieve their dreams of employment in their desired profession.

The experience and skills I gained from nursing abroad, as well as my experience with the NHS, made my job as a clinical skills tutor at the university truly enjoyable. Initially, I had some anxiety about being an overseas nurse on a visa and whether I would be accepted in the higher education environment. However, I soon learned that having the right skills and knowledge about a particular speciality can take you far in life. If you are reading this book and struggling with making the decision to apply for your dream job, my advice to you is to go for it and don't look back! It is important to note that while there may be challenges along the way, with determination and perseverance, anything is possible.

As of the time of writing this book, I am proud to say that I am one of the senior lecturers in International and Adult Nursing in the Faculty of Health, Education, Medicine, and Social Care at one of the most esteemed universities in the UK. My hard work and dedication to my field have not gone unnoticed, as I was featured as Alumni of the Month in 2016. Being recognised by your university is a great feeling, and it serves as a reminder that your hard work has paid off.

If you plan on becoming an international student in the UK, there are several important things you should be aware of before starting the process. One of the most crucial aspects is determining when to apply for a visa to leave your home country and travel to the UK. To summarise, the key points to consider will be discussed in the next section of this book.

Why study in the UK?

The United Kingdom (UK) has established a solid reputation for its universities and higher education system. While there may be other universities around the world that provide better teaching, it is hard to overlook the fact that the UK offers a higher average salary than many other international communities, a more enriching university experience than my home country, and arguably, a more fun and abundant social life. Studying abroad offers a unique opportunity to learn about different cultures and ways of life. It is one thing to read about it, but it is an entirely different experience to come and live it yourself. There is a level of personal growth and development that can only be achieved by immersing oneself in a new culture. The UK is an ideal destination for international students who want to broaden their horizons and gain a unique perspective on life. Additionally, studying in the UK allows students to meet people from all over the world, expanding their network and enhancing their global understanding.

Packing your suitcase

Moving to a foreign country can be a life-changing experience that opens up new horizons and helps you grow as a person. However, it requires careful planning and preparation to make sure that everything goes smoothly. One of the most important things you need to do is to sort out your visa requirements, which can vary depending on the country you are moving to. You should research the process thoroughly and make sure you have all the necessary documents and paperwork in order.

When it comes to packing your suitcase, it's essential to think carefully about what you will need in your new home. In addition to clothing and personal items, you should also include any important documents such as your passport, visa, and other legal paperwork. It's a good idea to make copies of these documents and keep them in a safe place, as well as having digital backups in case the originals get lost or stolen.

Another critical aspect of moving to a foreign country is adapting to the local culture and customs. You should research the region's climate and weather conditions to ensure you pack appropriate clothing and footwear. You should also research the cultural norms and customs of the country you are moving to, as these can vary widely from country to country. It's important to be respectful of local customs and to make an effort to learn the language and communicate effectively with locals.

Overall, moving abroad can be a daunting task, but with careful planning and preparation, it can also be an incredibly rewarding experience that broadens your horizons and helps you grow as a person.

Food and clothing

When travelling to the UK, it is not uncommon for people to bring foodstuffs from their home countries. This can be a great way to satisfy any

Author's Personal Experience

cravings you may have for the tastes of home, particularly if you are unfamiliar with the kind of food available in the UK. However, it is important to note that bringing foodstuffs and liquids can cause issues at customs, especially if you are travelling to another continent and studying abroad.

It is recommended that you carefully read up on what foodstuffs are allowed on the plane and at your final destination to avoid having your food confiscated. Different countries have different regulations regarding the transportation of foodstuffs, and it is important to be aware of these regulations to avoid any issues with customs officials.

Some common items that may be restricted or prohibited include fresh fruits and vegetables, meat products, dairy products, and certain types of nuts and seeds. It is also important to note that some countries may have restrictions on the quantity of foodstuffs that can be brought in, so it is essential to check the regulations carefully before packing your bags.

By taking a bit of time to research the regulations and restrictions regarding the transportation of foodstuffs, you can avoid any unpleasant surprises and ensure that your travels are as smooth and stress-free as possible.

When packing for a trip, it is important to consider the weather conditions of the destination. This is particularly true for the UK, where the weather is notoriously unpredictable. If you do not plan well, you may end up carrying clothing that you may not use, which can be a waste of space in your suitcase. To ensure that you are well-prepared for any weather condition, it is recommended that you pack layers of clothing. This way, you can easily adjust your clothes according to the weather.

Author's Personal Experience

In the UK, it rains a lot, so it is essential to layer up. You should consider packing clothes that can be easily layered, such as t-shirts, sweaters, and jackets. On a typical day at a university in the UK, students have to walk around a lot, so it is crucial to wear comfortable shoes. You may consider casual boots, trainers, or sandals, depending on your preference. It is best to avoid wearing heels unless you are comfortable walking in them for extended periods.

If you want to pull off a casual look, you should pack many pairs of jeans and/or denim skirts. These are versatile and suitable for different occasions. When going to lectures or exploring the city with friends, most students prefer wearing coats and jackets. A comfortable hoodie or an oversized jacket is also a popular choice. These provide warmth and comfort, which are essential when spending long hours outside.

Finally, you should carry a decent-sized shoulder bag with you to accommodate books, a laptop, and stationery. This way, you can keep your hands free and avoid carrying heavy bags. A shoulder bag is also a stylish accessory that can complement your outfit and make you look fashionable.

Dress tips for attending formal events

As part of their academic journey, students are often required to attend various formal events throughout their courses. These events may take many forms, such as seminars, award ceremonies, or presentations, and are typically attended by faculty, staff, and other students. It is crucial to dress appropriately for these occasions to make a good impression, so it's a good idea to plan ahead and add some suitable clothing to your packing list. Wearing smart and presentable attire can help you feel more confident and professional, and it demonstrates respect for the event and the people attending. So, whether it's a formal blazer, a dress shirt, a pair of dress shoes, or a modest dress, make sure to pack something that will help you look your best and feel comfortable during these important academic events.

Days spent at university

Studying in a UK university can be quite different from studying in your home country. Unlike the traditional five-day-a-week schedule, university days in the UK are typically only two to three days per week. This allows students to have more flexibility in their schedules and gives them the opportunity to engage in other activities, like part-time jobs, internships, or extracurricular activities.

To ensure that students understand what is expected of them in each module, the university provides a Module Guide that outlines all the relevant information. This guide includes details on the module's curriculum, what the student needs to do to pass it, and how the module will be assessed.

In addition to the Module Guide, students also have access to a virtual learning environment called the CANVAS page or (VLE). This platform provides easy access to all the information needed for self-directed learning. It includes lecture notes, reading materials, and other resources that students can use to enhance their learning experience.

While some information will be communicated in class, it is strongly recommended that students engage with the CANVAS page, as not everything will be covered in face-to-face interactions with their tutors. By actively using this platform, students can better prepare themselves for their assessments and maximise their learning outcomes.

Study skills support

Developing strong academic skills is key to achieving academic success and approaching assessments with confidence while reducing stress levels. As a former international student myself, I can attest to the challenges of writing essays in the UK education system. However, universities offer a wealth of study skills support that includes a variety of workshops, self-directed online resources, and appointments with academic advisers. These resources can provide a solid foundation for independent learning at any level of university study. They can help you to improve your grades, enhance your academic abilities, and achieve your full potential. Whether you're struggling with academic writing, time management, or exam preparation, these resources can give you the tools and techniques you need to succeed. So, if you're looking to improve your academic skills and achieve your goals, take advantage of the support available to you at your university.

Student services

At university, there are various teams of specialists whose primary goal is to provide all-round support to students. They work tirelessly to help students develop the skills and competencies they'll need for their future careers. These teams are always available to offer any assistance students may require during their time at the university. Whether it's academic support, career guidance, mental health counselling, or financial advice, these teams are there to ensure that students have everything they need to succeed in their academic pursuits and beyond.

Author's Personal Experience

Working to pay your bills whilst studying in the UK

If you are an international student planning to study in the UK, it is important to know that a student visa issued for a full-time degree programme enables you to work part-time for a maximum of 20 hours per week during term time. However, it is essential to understand that relying solely on part-time work to fund your studies may not be the best approach. It is recommended that you do not depend completely on part-time work to pay for your tuition fees and living expenses while studying in the UK.

It is vital for students to have enough financial resources to cover their tuition fees and living expenses for the entire duration of their studies. The 20-hour work limit includes any paid or unpaid work for one or more organisations in any one week. It is important to comply with this limit to avoid any legal issues or penalties.

However, this is an excellent opportunity for international students to gain valuable work experience while studying in the UK. The international student advice team at the university can provide you with more information about the rules and regulations governing part-time work for international students. They can also guide you on how to find part-time work opportunities that align with your course schedule and academic commitments.

In conclusion, while part-time work can provide some financial support, it is strongly recommended that students do not rely solely on it to fund their studies. It is important to plan and budget accordingly to ensure you have enough financial resources to cover your expenses during your stay in the UK.

Author's Personal Experience

Feeling homesick

Feeling homesick is a common experience that many students face, particularly those who are leaving home for the first time. It is something that you may encounter as an international student, even if you are from the UK. However, it is important to remember that these feelings will not last forever and that you will eventually adjust to your new surroundings. It is okay to cry if you feel homesick, and you should not feel ashamed if you do. It is a natural reaction to being away from home and your loved ones.

If you are struggling with homesickness, there are things you can do to help alleviate your feelings. One thing that may help is to call home and speak with your loved ones. Hearing their voices and knowing that they are still there for you can provide comfort and reassurance.

Another strategy that may be helpful is to surround yourself with reminders of home. You could create a playlist of songs that remind you of home, display photos of loved ones in your room, or watch a TV series or movie that you used to enjoy back home. These things may help you feel more connected to your home and reduce your feelings of homesickness.

Ultimately, being an international student is an amazing opportunity that you will cherish for the rest of your life. Although it may be challenging at times, remember that you are not alone in your experiences and resources are available to help you through this transition period. When you feel homesick, remind yourself why you chose to go abroad. You'll be so proud of yourself for taking that bold step. After all, it is not going to last forever, so make the most of it. Today, I am so proud of the effort and sacrifice I made, and my family is very proud of me. Also, identify your religious community depending on your faith and get involved. They can be very supportive physically, emotionally and spiritually. You can have prayer partners and fun partners who will continue to encourage your effort and make you feel less lonely. This worked for me.

Social etiquette observed in the UK

When you leave your home country to pursue your studies in a foreign land, you become an ambassador of your country. This means that your actions and behaviour will reflect upon your nation in the international community. You are likely to spend a considerable amount of time in British society and interact with its people on numerous occasions. During your stay, it is important to conduct yourself in a manner that promotes your personality and enhances your life skills. Understanding the customs and etiquette of British society will help you appreciate and respect the social norms in Britain and adapt to the new environment smoothly.

In Britain, politeness is highly valued, and it is considered a key aspect of their culture. Therefore, it is advisable to incorporate certain phrases such as 'Thank you,' 'I'm sorry,' 'Please,' and 'Excuse me' into your British vocabulary. Using these phrases regularly will help you to be courteous and respectful in your interactions with the locals. It is always better to be overly polite than to be perceived as rude or impolite. By showing respect and kindness towards others, you will be able to create a positive impression and build long-lasting relationships in British society.

University etiquette

- **Punctuality.** When it comes to punctuality, it's important to keep in mind that

Author's Personal Experience

arriving on time is a crucial aspect of British culture. Whether it is at the start of the day, after breaks, or for meetings and appointments, it's expected that you arrive at least five minutes before the scheduled time. This can be a significant shift for some international students who may come from cultures where arriving early is not always necessary, and people tend to let others go first. This relaxed attitude towards punctuality is sometimes referred to as "African time" in some parts of the world. However, in the UK, it is customary for events to start on time, and arriving late without a valid reason is generally frowned upon.

If you do happen to be late for a meeting or appointment, it is important to offer a polite apology while taking ownership of your mistake. On the other hand, if you know you're going to be late, it is always a good idea to call ahead and let the other person know. This shows consideration for their time and can help prevent any unnecessary delays or inconvenience. Overall, being punctual is an essential part of showing respect for others and is highly valued in British culture.

- **Respect.** In order to maintain a positive and respectful learning environment, it is important to keep in mind a few key principles. First and foremost, it is essential that you treat your classmates, teachers, and school property with respect. This means refraining from any actions or language that could be considered hurtful or disrespectful. Additionally, it is important to be kind and polite at all times. This includes using positive language and practising good manners, such as saying "please" and "thank you" and holding doors open for others when appropriate.

Author's Personal Experience

When engaging in group discussions or conversations, it is important to avoid talking over people. Instead, wait until someone has finished their statement before speaking. If you do need to interrupt someone, be sure to do so politely and apologise for doing so. Interrupting someone who is still speaking can be seen as rude and disrespectful, so it's important to be mindful of this. By following these guidelines and striving to be courteous and respectful in all your interactions, you can help create a positive and productive learning environment where everyone feels valucd and appreciated. Be kind and polite, use positive language and be courteous to others. Do not talk over people; wait until someone finishes their statements before you speak. When you have to interrupt someone, apologise nicely for doing so. It is rather rude to interrupt someone who is still speaking.

- **Respect someone's personal space** by keeping your hands and feet to yourself (do not touch without asking and getting consent). It is important to respect someone's personal space by keeping your hands and feet to yourself. It is always advisable to seek consent before touching someone, as it can be perceived as intrusive and offensive. This is particularly true for British people, who value their personal space and prefer to keep a fair distance when in conversation. However, this may be different for international students who come from backgrounds where touching and pointing at people while communicating is a natural part of their culture. While this may not be a big deal in some cultures, it is essential to learn about the norms of the host culture and adjust accordingly.

Author's Personal Experience

For instance, I come from a cultural background where touching and pointing while communicating is acceptable and even considered enjoyable. However, I have learned to keep my hands to myself since learning about the English culture's emphasis on respecting personal space. I have realised that in certain situations, it is necessary to ask for permission before touching someone, even in intimate relationships. This can be surprising for those who come from cultures where such behaviour is acceptable. However, it is essential to learn about the culture and norms of the people around you to avoid misunderstandings and ensure respectful interactions.

- **Do not use your phone.** Mobile phones have become an indispensable aspect of our lives that has revolutionised the way we communicate and acquire information. However, excessive use of smartphones and other mobile devices can have a negative impact on our lives. Studies suggest that overuse of such devices can lead to several issues, including the deterioration of interpersonal relationships. Ironically, despite being a tool for communication, technology can actually lead to disconnection between people, a phenomenon known as phubbing or "phone snubbing".

Phubbing can be detrimental to personal relationships, especially romantic relationships. It can also harm your bond with your children. The habit of looking at your phone rather than interacting with the people around you can damage your relationship with your partner, leading to feelings of neglect and separation. Research has shown that the use of mobile phones during mealtime or while spending time with family and friends can create a sense of disconnection and dissatisfaction.

Therefore, it is essential to be mindful of phone usage and limit it during certain situations, like family gatherings, meals, or romantic evenings. It is advised to turn your phone off during important meetings or at least turn off the ringer completely and put the phone away. If you are expecting an important call during such occasions, inform the people around you beforehand to avoid any misunderstandings. By doing so, you can avoid phubbing and ensure that you are fully present in the moment with the people around you.

- **Emails.** Email is a very common mode of communication at university, in the workplace and socially. It's important to get the tone and style of your email right, as this will help you make a good impression and hopefully get the response you are looking for.

The subject line should be simple to reflect your email, e.g. 'Request for tutorial.'

Use an appropriate salutation, starting your email with 'Dear' or 'Hello.' 'Hey' is not appropriate when writing to your tutor, but it could be when writing to a friend. Also, address the recipient suitably. Many years ago, as an international student, I made the mistake of addressing my tutors as Sir, Ma, mam, Mrs, etc., because that was the normal way I addressed my tutors in my home country. I have learned that it is best to avoid gendered addresses like 'Mr' or 'Mrs'. Some lecturers and tutors might allow you to address them by their first name, but it is better to wait until they have told you that is how they would prefer you address them. In some cases, you can call your tutor or lecturer by their first name if they have routinely used their first name only to sign off on emails sent to students.

Author's Personal Experience

Introduce yourself. Tell your tutor who you are, especially if this is the first time you have written to them. They may have hundreds of other students also emailing them.

Keep your email short and straight to the point. End it with a set phrase such as 'Kind regards,' 'Best wishes,' or 'Thank you,' followed by your name. Always communicate using your student email account when communicating with your tutors. This is university policy. Lastly, always proofread your email before sending it!

> **Useful tip**: Always think about your audience (who you're writing to) and your aim (what you want). This will help you work out how formal you need to be and how much background information you might need to provide. It will leave the reader with a great impression of your communication skills.

Public place etiquette

- **Queuing.** Queue up in line to get served; do not break the order or jump up the queue. In the UK, you will find an orderly queue wherever there is a mass of people, for example, waiting to pay in a shop. British etiquette dictates that when you arrive, you join the back of the queue so that each person receives the service in the order that they arrived. When boarding a bus, train or ferry, form an orderly line. Do not budge or push. Remember, personal space needs to be respected. This is very different from where I come from. As an international student many years ago, I used to wonder why there were spaces between people queuing, and I felt the urge to fill that gap. Where I come from, queuing is a different ball game. It is fondly called bumper-to-bumper! With no space whatsoever, LOL. Now I know better.

- **Let passengers on public transport exit first.** It is important to practise proper etiquette when using public transportation. One of the most important rules to follow is to allow passengers who wish to exit the vehicle to do so first. Please make sure that you give them enough space and do not block their way. It is also important to wait until the exiting passengers have completely cleared the way before attempting to board the vehicle. This will ensure that everyone can move in a safe and efficient manner and that no one gets unnecessarily delayed or inconvenienced. Thank you for your cooperation in making public transportation a pleasant experience for everyone.

- **Keep moving.** When you are walking on a busy pavement, it is important to keep moving to avoid blocking the way for other pedestrians. Similarly, when you are filing into a stadium or shopping at a crowded local supermarket, try to keep the flow of people moving smoothly by not stopping abruptly. If you need to take a phone call, find a quiet and less crowded spot where you can step aside without disrupting the movement of others. Remember, being considerate and aware of your surroundings can help make the experience more pleasant for everyone.

- **Using mobile phones.** When using your mobile phone in public, it is important to be mindful of those around you. Generally, it is best to maintain a buffer of at least ten feet to conduct a semi-private call without disturbing anyone nearby. If you need to make or take a call when you're in a crowded area, it's best to keep it brief and as quiet as possible. This is because using your phone on loudspeaker in public can be disruptive to those around you. The sound can be loud and make it difficult for others to have conversations or focus on their own tasks. It can also be considered impolite because it is a public display of your phone usage and can be perceived as an attempt to draw attention to yourself and your device. In addition, you should be aware that others may be listening in on your conversation, which can be a violation of your privacy. Therefore, it's always best to use discretion when using your mobile phone in public spaces.

- **Consider noise levels.** It is important to be mindful of the noise you generate in public spaces, as others may not share the same level of enthusiasm as you. This includes speaking loudly, yelling, laughing, playing music, and talking on your mobile phone. While it's perfectly natural to chat with a friend in person, it's important to keep in mind the volume and tone of your conversation, especially if it's too loud and disruptive to others around you. When using your phone on speaker, it can be even more challenging to control the volume, and others may not be able to move away from it, making it even more important to be considerate of your surroundings.

- **Hold the door for those behind you**, especially when they are within a few steps of it. Whoever gets to the door first should open it. If someone holds the door for you, acknowledge their kindness with eye contact, a smile, and a genuine "Thank you."

Author's Personal Experience

For the person holding the door open, it can give them a sense of happiness and the rewarding feeling that they're helping someone. For the person going through the door, it can make them look at you more positively and feel appreciated. It is a kind action to do and can help make someone's day!

I remember holding the door open for all of my classes, and although I did not get many "Thank yous" *(but perhaps I should have done!)*, I found that I did not need them. The fulfilment of doing something kind, particularly when we live in the world that we do, was enough for me. By doing this, I knew I was making a small but tangible difference to my class and the way they felt. I hoped it would inspire others to do the same, which, if they did, would help to make the world kinder. The best part? When I did get a thank you, it filled me with a glow of happiness inside me that was addictive; I wanted to repeat it again.

- **Lift doors.** When you're using a lift, it is important to be considerate of others who may also need to use it. If you see someone running towards the lift as the doors are closing, hold the door open for them or press the open door button to keep the doors from closing. This small gesture can make a big difference and help to create a more friendly and welcoming environment for everyone. Remember, a little bit of kindness can go a long way.

- **Staring and pointing.** Do not stare or point your finger at anyone. As in most countries, pointing at someone with just your index finger is rude in the UK. You should usually use an open hand with the palm up and all four fingers pointing towards the person. Holding up your fist with the back of your hand facing the other person and raising just your middle finger is one of the most aggressive/offensive gestures in English. Basically, it is swearing, meaning "F*ck you," and is often a replacement for actually hitting someone. Don't allow your behaviour to disturb others; make an effort to be considerate of them.

- **Do not pick your nose in public.** Maintaining personal hygiene is crucial for good health, and one essential aspect of it is cleaning the nose. If you feel the need to clear your nostrils, using a handkerchief is an effective way to do so. However, it's worth noting that this practice is considered mildly taboo in most cultures, and people usually prefer to do it in private. Nose-picking is a prevalent habit worldwide, but it's also a potentially embarrassing and socially unacceptable behaviour. Even though most people engage in it, observing someone else doing it can trigger a sense of disgust in many individuals. Therefore, it's best to keep this activity discreet and maintain proper etiquette in public settings.

- **Do not burp in public.** Burping in public is generally considered impolite and disrespectful in the UK. If you happen to burp unintentionally, it is recommended to cover your mouth with your hand and say "Excuse me" afterwards. However, it is always best to try to avoid burping in public as much as possible. If you must burp, try to do so discreetly and apologise immediately afterwards. This will show that you are respectful of those around you and aware of social norms. Remember, good manners go a long way in making a positive impression on others.

- **Do not throw rubbish away.** It is important to be responsible for the waste we generate and the impact it has on the environment. One way to do this is by not throwing rubbish away in the streets or countryside. Instead, we should find a suitable bin nearby to dispose of it properly. If you cannot find a bin nearby, it is best to carry the rubbish with you until you can dispose of it correctly.

It is worth noting that putting your rubbish in someone else's bin is not acceptable and is considered a form of anti-social behaviour. In fact, it is technically illegal and falls under the category of fly-tipping. This act is commonly referred to as 'bin stuffing' within the waste industry. Even though many people may not be aware of this, it is essential to ensure that we dispose of our waste responsibly and appropriately.

Moreover, discarding cigarette butts in the streets is not only a nuisance, but can also cause problems. Therefore, it is crucial to put the cigarette out and dispose of it in a cigarette bin or other appropriate waste receptacle. By doing so, we can help keep our environment clean and safe for everyone.

- **Do not spit in open spaces.** It is important to remember that spitting or urinating in public spaces is not only disrespectful but also a criminal offence in the UK. Anyone caught doing so could be issued with an on-the-spot fine ranging from £80 to £100, known as a Fixed Penalty Notice. This is because spitting and urinating are both types of littering and can be harmful to the environment. If you are reported for spitting or urinating in public, you will be asked to complete a report litter form.

It is important to use a paper towel or tissue to catch your spit and immediately dispose of it in a bin. Do not litter the streets with your saliva. Similarly, urinating in public is unacceptable and can cause a public nuisance. Therefore, it is important to use public toilets whenever possible and avoid urinating in open spaces. By being mindful of the consequences of spitting and urinating in public areas, we can help maintain a cleaner and safer environment for everyone.

- **Do not pass wind loudly**, and try to pass it far away from others. Flatulence arises surprisingly often in legal cases. It figures prominently in disability, human rights and employment law cases. But it did not seem to be the subject of criminal proceedings until recently. In 2020, the police charged someone for farting in

Austria. He was fined 500 euros for loudly breaking wind after officers stopped him to check his identity. They justified the arrest by stating that the young man had been "provocative and uncooperative." How so? Well, they said that he had "slightly raised himself from the bench, looked at the officers and patently, in a completely deliberate way, emitted a massive flatulence in their immediate proximity." I cannot help laughing out loud at this information!

- **Do not cough/yawn/sneeze without covering your mouth.** Cover your mouth and nose with a tissue when you cough or sneeze. Throw used tissues into a rubbish bin. If you don't have a tissue, cough or sneeze into your elbow, not your hands. It is not just a demonstration of good manners to cover your cough. Doing so helps reduce the spread of germs, including the highly contagious influenza virus. The flu and some other infections are spread through microscopic water droplets expelled from an infected person, commonly through coughing, sneezing, and hand-to-mouth contact.

Dining etiquette

Calling for service. Do not wave or yell to call over a waiter or person of service. You should address your waiter or waitress with "Sir, Miss, Ms, or Ma'am" as appropriate. If they introduce themselves by name, use their names. Or you may keep an eye out for them until they make eye contact and then nod or raise your hand. You may also gently say, "Excuse me" as they pass by. DO NOT whistle, snap your fingers, clap your hands, whistle, or call, "Hey, you!" Being rude to a waiter indicates that a person cannot earn respect easily but instead demands it. This is not a characteristic that one would look for in a leader.

What to put on the table. When it comes to table etiquette, it's important to remember not to place bags, purses, sunglasses, mobile phones, or briefcases on the table. It may seem like a small detail, but it can make a big difference in how others perceive you. Dining etiquette is about more than just table manners – it's about showing respect for the people you're dining with and making them feel comfortable.

For those who are new to dining etiquette, it can be a bit overwhelming at first. When I first arrived in the UK, I wasn't familiar with all the customs and practices that were expected of me. I'm sure my friends must have put up with a lot of inappropriate behaviour from me in the beginning. But over time, I learned what was expected of me and how to conduct myself in a polite and respectful manner. By following these simple rules of etiquette, you can show others that you value their company and that you're committed to making the dining experience as enjoyable as possible.

Napkin etiquette. When it comes to napkin etiquette, there are a few things to keep in mind. Firstly, upon seating, it's customary to place the napkin in your lap. This is to keep your clothes clean and free from any food debris that may fall during the meal. When the meal is finished, it's important to fold your napkin neatly and place it to the left of your place setting. This signals to the server that you have finished your meal and they can clear your plate. However, it's worth noting that some cultural traditions may differ in terms of napkin placement. For example, in some regions, it is common to place the napkin on the chest while eating. Regardless of the cultural differences, the most important thing is to be respectful and mindful of the customs and traditions of those around you.

Sharing food. When dining in a group and sharing food, it is important to prioritise the needs of others. One way to do this is by offering to serve food to those seated around you before serving yourself. Additionally, it is important to be mindful of the amount of food you take, ensuring that you do not take more than you can eat, and leaving enough for others. Taking small portions and being considerate of others' needs will help ensure that everyone can enjoy the food and have a positive dining experience. By following these guidelines, you can help create a pleasant and respectful atmosphere during shared meals.

When to start eating. When dining with others, it is important to be mindful of your table manners. One such manner is to wait until everyone has been served their food before you start eating. It is customary in the UK to begin eating only after everyone has been served, as it is considered extremely rude to start eating before others.

In an ideal situation, the kitchen should plan and prepare all the dishes to be ready at the same time. This ensures that everyone can enjoy their meal together, without anyone feeling left out or rushed. If, for any reason, you are served your meal before others, it is still best to wait until everyone is served before you begin eating. This shows respect and consideration for your fellow diners and helps to create a comfortable and enjoyable dining experience for all.

Positioning the cutlery. When it comes to dining etiquette, it's important to pay attention to the positioning of your cutlery. In most cultures, including the UK, it is customary to rest your cutlery on the sides of your plate between mouthfuls and to place them together in the centre when you are finished. This not only helps to keep your eating area tidy, but it also signals to your dining companions that you are taking care to observe social norms and show respect for the meal and those around you. It's interesting to note that this practice may vary depending on the cultural context, and it's worth taking the time to learn about the dining customs of different regions and communities, particularly if you plan to travel or dine with individuals from diverse backgrounds.

Chewing. Regarding dining etiquette, there are a few rules that are universally accepted and expected. One of the most important ones is to chew with your mouth closed and avoid talking with food in your mouth. This means that when you take a bite of food, your lips should be firmly shut while you chew and swallow it delicately. It is considered impolite and unhygienic to eat with your mouth open, and it is often considered worse than other common dining faux pas, like putting your elbows on the table or holding your fork in the wrong hand.

To avoid any embarrassing situations, it is recommended to take small mouthfuls and keep your mouth closed while you chew. It is also important to avoid eating noisily, as this can be a major distraction for others at the table. In the UK, people tend to eat very quietly, almost silently, so if you are dining in a British setting, it is best to follow suit and avoid making any unnecessary noise while eating.

Overall, practising good table manners is an essential part of dining etiquette, and following these basic rules will help ensure that you make a good impression and enjoy a pleasant meal with others.

Leaving the table. When you are staying with a homestay, it is important to be mindful of the cultural norms around meal times. Generally, it is polite to wait until everyone has finished eating or until you are told it is okay to leave the table. If, for some reason, you need to leave the table before everyone else has finished, you can politely ask if it is okay to be excused. Remember to always be respectful and considerate of your hosts and their customs.

Giving thanks. Always remember to thank your host. When you're invited to a dinner party, it's always a good idea to show appreciation to your host for their efforts in making the evening enjoyable. A simple gesture like saying "thank you" can go a long way in making your host feel valued and appreciated. You may express your gratitude by complimenting them on the meal that they prepared, acknowledging the effort they put into the decorations, or thanking them for making you feel welcome in their home. For instance, you could say something like, "I just wanted to take a moment to express my gratitude for the amazing dinner and wonderful evening we had at your home. The food was delicious, and the ambience you created was simply amazing. You truly have a gift for hosting, and I'm grateful to have been a part of it all." Remember, showing appreciation is not only polite but also a great way to strengthen relationships and foster a sense of community.

Social etiquette

Greetings. Hello there! In the United Kingdom, the most prevalent way of greeting someone is by shaking hands firmly. This gesture is typically employed when meeting someone for the first time or on formal occasions. When it comes to greeting close friends or family members, hugging and kissing on the cheek are more commonly used. It's worth noting that the number of kisses on the cheek can vary depending on the region. While some areas opt for one kiss, others may go for two or even three.

Hello or hi. These are common verbal greetings, and you're also likely to hear "Alright?" which means hello and is not a question. Where I come from, "Are you alright?" could mean two things: either you have done something wrong, and they are checking if something is wrong with your brain, or they are just checking on your well-being. You identify the difference by the tone of voice used to ask the question and hand gestures pointing to the head of the person asking. I am sure some international students can relate to this information. LOL!

Mind your P's (please) and Q's (thank yous). "Please" and "Thank you" are two of the most common phrases in the UK, and it is important to use them when appropriate. Please is a word used in the English language to indicate

Author's Personal Experience

politeness and respect while making a request. Saying please is a sign that someone is recognising another person's worth as a fellow human being, regardless of their station in life. Not saying please when you make a request in the UK can be seen as being very rude.

I remember the first day I tried to buy a bus ticket in the UK. I was asking the bus driver to give me a return ticket without saying the magic word, *"Please."* The bus driver kept me standing for a while without giving me the ticket. I wondered why and what was happening until he sarcastically said to me, *"Do you have the word please where you come from?"* This was one of my embarrassing moments, LOL! So, if you are new to the UK and reading this book, please do not forget to say please and thank you to avoid such awkward moments.

Asking questions. In British culture, asking questions that are too personal, difficult, or uncomfortable to someone you do not have a close relationship with is generally considered impolite. Such questions may range from inquiring about one's political stance, sexual orientation, religious beliefs, or income level. In particular, discussing money is a sensitive topic that many British people find uncomfortable and may perceive as rude. As a result, it is advisable to exercise caution and sensitivity when broaching such topics, especially with people you do not know well.

Apologising. When you accidentally bump into someone, it's always a good idea to say "Sorry" as a common courtesy. Even if it was not entirely your fault, apologising can help diffuse any tension and prevent an argument from escalating. It is a habit that can be seen as very amusing by someone who is not familiar with this cultural norm. So, the next time you accidentally bump into someone, don't hesitate to apologise. It is a small gesture that can go a long way in making the situation better.

Physical contact with friends. In the UK, physical contact between friends can vary depending on the gender and cultural norms. For instance, holding hands as friends is not a common practice. Instead, it is more typical for female friends to link arms while walking together. This gesture is seen as a sign of closeness and friendship, rather than a romantic gesture. However, for male friends, physical contact is usually limited, and there is generally no contact between them. This is not because of any negative connotations attached to it, but rather a cultural norm that has been passed down over generations. Therefore, it is important to keep in mind that physical contact between friends can vary significantly depending on the cultural context and gender.

Make eye contact. One effective way to demonstrate that you are actively listening and engaged in a conversation is by maintaining eye contact with the speaker. However, certain cultures and societies view eye contact differently. For instance, in some cultures, it is considered impolite to look directly into the eyes of someone who holds a higher status or authority than you. This can be a significant cultural shock for people who come from societies where avoiding eye contact is perceived as a sign of disrespect.

For instance, I come from a culture where they were taught to avoid making eye contact with their boss during conversations as a sign of respect. However, when I moved to a different culture where eye contact is considered an essential aspect of communication, I found it challenging to adapt to this new cultural norm. However, too much eye contact can be seen as aggressive or a sexual come-on. It is best to make direct eye contact that breaks away now and again. Prolonged eye contact can make people feel uncomfortable, and staring is impolite. If talking to a group, be sure to make equal eye contact with all who are present.

Courtesy. British people are known for their strong cultural emphasis on politeness and courtesy. One aspect of this cultural trait is that they tend to use polite requests rather than direct orders or instructions. When asking someone to do something, they will often frame it as a question rather than a command. For example, instead of saying, "Come over here," a British person might say, "Do you want to come over to this side, please?" This is intended to be a subtle way of communicating that the person should come over without sounding too pushy or aggressive.

However, this can be a bit confusing for people from other cultures who are used to more direct communication styles. In some cultures, including where I come from, it is common to give direct commands and instructions without using polite language. This can be perceived as rude or impolite in the UK, where people value courtesy and politeness in their interactions with others. It is important to be aware of these cultural differences and adjust your communication style accordingly when interacting with people from different backgrounds.

Strangers calling you sweetheart, honey, love, etc.

In Britain, you will often find terms used for complimenting loved ones used casually among strangers, e.g., the waiter in the restaurant, the taxi driver taking you to work, or the woman who works in the baker's shop. It may surprise you, but they'll often use these terms as a kind of casual, friendly greeting. It doesn't mean they're in love with you; they're just trying to be nice!

Author's Personal Experience

Some of the most commonly used terms and their meaning may include:

Love/luv

The term love in Britain is often written as luv, and it gets used simply as a title most of the time. For example, if a woman runs into a man in the street, he might say, "Watch where you're going, luv!" Similarly, if you walk into a café, whether you're a man or a woman, the waitress might ask, "What are you having, luv?" It is a word that's more often used to address strangers among the working and middle classes and not typically among the upper classes.

Because love is used regularly in everyday conversation, it's very easy to transfer across when speaking to a partner, meaning many call their loved one love, usually at the end of sentences. For example, "How was your day, love?" or "Hello, love, would you like a cup of tea?"

Honey/hun

This is another word that tends to get shortened slightly in common usage, which happens often with terms of affection. Honey is a word that is typically used between couples but rarely by strangers. It's far more common to hear the word hun used when someone you don't know is talking to you, similar to luv. "What can I get you, hun?"

It is not unusual to find words relating to sweet foods used as terms of endearment, like sugar and honey pie.

Sweetheart

Another term that involves sweetness, sweetheart, is used as a term of affection between loved ones and also as a familiar term of address, like hun or luv. It can be traced all the way back to the 13th century, originating from the Middle English term, *swete hert*. Because doctors knew little about our hearts and circulatory systems back then, figurative words were attached to the heart regarding people's personalities, like heavy-hearted, light-hearted, and cold-hearted. As love makes us giddy, often our hearts beat faster, and so the term *swete hert* came about to mean a fast-beating heart. The term slowly changed into sweetheart – often used to address someone who makes your heart throb.

Meanwhile, as an international student in the UK, you do not have to feel pressured into using some of these terms for anyone you are not comfortable with. The best practice is to call people the names they want to be called!

Coping with challenges

According to recent surveys, students have reported using various self-help coping strategies to overcome the challenges they face. These strategies include but are not limited to talking about their problems with others, engaging in activities that they find useful or enjoyable, incorporating physical exercise into their routine, facing difficult situations with courage, maintaining a positive outlook towards life and participating in religious or spiritual activities that help them feel grounded.

In addition to these self-help strategies, mastering a handy skill can also prove to be very helpful. For instance, if you are good at cooking special food or making hair, you can make a lot of money while studying in the UK. It is never too early to start thinking about your future plans after completing your course. Start exploring your interests and passions, identify your strengths and weaknesses, and set goals that align with your aspirations. This will help you make the most of your time while studying and prepare you for a fulfilling career ahead.

Author's Personal Experience

What no one tells you about studying in the UK

You must read! As an international student in the UK, it is important to remember that reading written information thoroughly is crucial. It may be common for teachers in your home country to communicate important information verbally. However, in the UK, written instructions and guidelines are often the primary means of conveying information. It is vital to read all information provided in full, including any accompanying documents or attachments. Skipping sections or only reading the first and last paragraphs could result in misunderstandings or mistakes. By taking the time to read all written information carefully, you can ensure that you have a complete understanding of what is required of you and avoid any unnecessary errors.

You must write so many words yourself. It is an interesting fact that some international students come from a background where they have access to cybercafés that offer the service of typewriting their assignments or any piece of work by a professional. It may come as a surprise to them that in the UK, such business centres that provide such services do not exist. In the UK, it is a common practice to encourage everyone, including international students, to have a laptop and complete their written work themselves. This is because the universities and colleges in the UK place a great emphasis on academic integrity and originality of the work submitted by students. Therefore, it is expected that students write their own assignments, essays, and research papers, and any form of plagiarism is strictly prohibited. To maintain academic standards and integrity, the assessment criteria in the UK education system are designed to test the student's ability to present their thoughts and ideas in their own words, and not to rely on someone else to write for them.

No plagiarism. In academic writing, it is crucial to avoid plagiarism, which is the act of copying and pasting someone else's work without giving credit. Plagiarism is considered a serious offence in universities and can lead to severe consequences, including failing a course or expulsion. International students may find it challenging to develop academic writing skills that enable them to think critically and paraphrase effectively.

However, universities in the UK provide student support resources to help international students overcome these challenges. The Study Skills Plus team is a great resource that offers drop-in sessions for all students who need support with their academic writing skills. These sessions are designed to help students develop skills such as critical thinking, paraphrasing, and referencing, which are essential for producing original and high-quality academic work.

It is important to note that many universities also provide online resources and one-to-one support services for international students who may be struggling with academic writing. By taking advantage of these resources, international students can improve their academic writing skills and succeed in their studies.

Some practical tips to help students adjust

I understand that adjusting to university life can be an exciting yet challenging experience. Hence, to make this transition easier for students, I suggest the following practical tips:

Firstly, be prepared to feel homesick at times. It's normal to miss the comfort and familiarity of home, especially during the initial days. But remember that this feeling is temporary, and things will get better with time.

Secondly, take part in orientation activities on campus, which is an excellent opportunity to get a feel for the university environment and meet new people. Orientation sessions are designed to provide crucial information about the university and the resources available to students. It's also an excellent way to connect with other students who are in the same boat as you.

Thirdly, joining social clubs, volunteering groups, and extracurricular activities can be a fantastic way to meet new people, get involved, and make a difference. You can also connect with students from your own culture or similar courses of study, which can help you feel more at home. I suggest joining WhatsApp groups to stay connected with your peers and receive important updates.

Fourthly, share your experiences with others who are in a similar situation. It's an excellent way to build a support system and connect with others who can relate to your situation.

Fifthly, university life involves a lot of independent study. You must learn to learn on your own and engage with all learning platforms like CANVAS, the library, Study Skills Plus, etc. Your teachers are genuinely interested in your learning and progress, and they may follow you up if you're not meeting your targets as expected. They can be very supportive and available to help when required, according to university policy and student charter.

Lastly, it is essential to remember that it gets easier when you get the hang of it. Once you settle into university life, your skills will improve, and you will enjoy carrying on and not want to go back home anytime soon. So, be patient, take one day at a time, and enjoy this new phase of your life.

Top mistakes international students make when studying in the UK

One of the common mistakes that international students make when studying in the UK is not considering the career options associated with the course they select. It's essential to understand that if you choose an expensive course, you need to know where it might lead you in the future. Unfortunately, some international students pick any available course without considering their career prospects and end up extending their visas. These students graduate with a PhD degree, but they often end up working in care homes as healthcare assistants or in other low-paying jobs that do not match their qualifications. While working in a care home or any other job is not bad, it is essential to recognise that, with a PhD degree, you could get a better graduate job with a higher salary and better prospects for growth. Therefore, it is crucial to think about your career aspirations before choosing a course to study. Doing so will help you make an informed decision that aligns with your career goals and aspirations. By considering your career options before selecting a course, you can set yourself up for a successful and fulfilling career in the UK.

Choosing a course just because they say it would get them a job. It is common for individuals to choose a course of study based solely on the promise of securing a job. However, it is essential to conduct thorough research to confirm the potential job prospects, likelihood of employment, and other pertinent factors. Obtaining a degree is only one of the many steps involved in acquiring a job. Factors such as relevant experiences, strong leadership skills, and previous achievements both within and outside of your course of study can significantly impact your employability. It is crucial to apply for positions that highlight your individual strengths, interests, and personality traits to increase your chances of securing a fulfilling and sustainable career. By taking the time to evaluate all of these factors, you can make informed decisions and achieve success in your chosen career path.

Not socialising with other people outside their language, nationality or country group, and just working 24/7. It is not uncommon for people to stick to socialising only with those who share their language, nationality, or cultural background, and focus solely on work. However, to become a better communicator, it is important to step out of your comfort zone and interact with people from different cultures and backgrounds. While it can be challenging to communicate in a language that is not your first, doing so will help you improve your language skills and broaden your worldview.

Studying in the UK offers a unique opportunity to meet people from all over the world and experience an international community. It's a great chance to make connections with people, learn about their cultures, and gain a better understanding of the world. By embracing this opportunity, you'll be able to expand your horizons and develop skills that will benefit you both personally and professionally.

Lack of formation of professional relationships. One of the biggest obstacles to professional growth and advancement is the lack of formation of professional relationships. It is important to attend educational and professional conferences and workshops where you can meet potential future colleagues, mentors or even a future boss. These events provide excellent opportunities to network with like-minded individuals in your field, learn from industry experts, and gain valuable insights into the latest trends and developments.

It is understandable that you may have other commitments or responsibilities that can sometimes make it difficult to attend social events or educational conferences. However, it's important to remember that the benefits of attending such events can be immense. For instance, you may miss out on valuable opportunities to connect with potential employers or clients, learn new skills, or gain industry knowledge.

It's also essential to prioritise your professional life over financial gain. While it's tempting to pick up every available shift, it is equally important to make time for networking and professional development. Attending social events and educational conferences may require you to invest time and money, but in the long run, it can pay off in terms of career growth and advancement.

So, always remember to strike a balance between your personal and professional commitments. While financial stability is important, it is equally essential to invest in your career by attending social events and educational conferences. You never know who you might meet or what opportunities may arise from these events.

Thinking that the post-study work visa is a quick solution. Many international students aspire to stay and work in their host country after their studies. One option available to them is to apply for a post-study work visa. However, some students may view this visa as an easy and immediate solution to their job search problems, without putting in the effort to improve their employability. They may simply want to continue with the same job they held during their studies without considering other opportunities that could enhance their careers.

It's important to note that obtaining a post-study work visa is just the first step in building a successful career. Students should also focus on networking with potential employers, improving their CVs, building a strong professional profile, and finding a sponsor who can support their skills and career aspirations. This requires dedication, hard work, and a willingness to go the extra mile to achieve one's goals.

While some students may prefer the easy way out, it is crucial to recognise that success requires effort and perseverance. By taking the time to develop their skills, build their network, and actively seek out new opportunities, international students can increase their chances of achieving their dreams and building a successful career in their host country.

Thinking that a lack of interview is due to your visa status or because you are not British. If you are someone who has ever felt that your visa status or non-British background has been the reason for not getting an interview, it is important to understand that it may not always be the case. While it is true that some employers might be hesitant to consider candidates with visa restrictions, it is not always the reason for not getting an interview call. In most cases, it is because your profile or CV is not strong enough to catch the employer's attention.

It is important to realise that people from diverse backgrounds get interviewed all the time, including those with visa restrictions. As a previous international student, I can say that I am a testimony to this fact. When I applied for a job as a lecturer at a university, I faced a lot of discouragement from my friends, who felt that my visa status would be a hindrance. However,

Author's Personal Experience

this was not the case. It was my strong CV and profile that helped me secure the job.

It is essential to showcase your strengths in your CV and cover letter so that you can make a lasting first impression on the employer. Remember that your CV is the first point of contact with the employer, so make it count. Highlight your skills, experience, and achievements in a way that convinces the employer that you are the right candidate for the job. And always remember that with hard work and perseverance, you can overcome any obstacle that comes your way.

Chapter Two

Culture Shocks and Stories from Lived Experience

This chapter delves into the various challenges and experiences international students face while studying in the UK. Culture, in this context, refers to everything that one must learn to behave in a way that is recognisable, predictable, and understandable to the people around them. "Culture shock" is the term used to describe the mixture of anxiety and feelings of confusion, excitement, and insecurity that individuals experience when they immerse themselves in a new culture. However, the intensity and duration of these feelings can vary from person to person.

Culture shock can manifest itself in several ways, such as communication problems, frustration, difficulty understanding the verbal and non-verbal communication of the host country, differences in food, weather, and more. Experts have identified four different phases of culture shock: the honeymoon stage, frustration stage, adjustment stage, and acceptance stage. While each person experiences these stages differently, they can provide a general guideline on how to adapt and cope with a new culture.

The honeymoon stage is characterised by feelings of intense happiness that can last for a week or several months. During this phase, you are on an exciting adventure, and you are enjoying learning about new people, foods, cultures, and experiences. This is an opportunity to make the most of your time, go out, explore, and truly immerse yourself in the new culture. The more you take advantage of this stage, the easier it can be to transition into the other stages of culture shock.

The frustration stage is characterised by feelings of irritability, anxiety, frustration, and even hostility. These feelings stem from being unable to understand things, such as being unable to speak or read the language on signs or menus. You may also start to miss things back home that were easy and familiar, including friends and family. This can manifest in physical symptoms of culture shock, such as excessive sleeping and isolation, as well as dissatisfaction with your new culture. It is important to speak to someone about your worries during this stage. The university usually has a counselling and well-being department where you can speak to someone, or you may have a personal tutor you could approach.

In **the adjustment stage**, you start to relax and develop a more balanced view of the new culture. Routine sets in, and life becomes more stable. You start to accept the different ways things are done and find ways to cope with the local culture to feel more comfortable and confident. This stage typically kicks in as you start to become familiar with the local culture, from foods and language to traditional customs.

The adaptation stage, also known as the "bicultural stage," is when you start to adapt and accept the new culture as your own. It is the phase in which you find acceptance of your new surroundings. You begin to feel like you belong and really understand and appreciate the culture that you're now a part of. This stage typically only kicks in once you're fully integrated into life. You have overcome the feelings of isolation and loneliness and now have new friends, activities to look forward to, new favourite foods, and more.

Patience Bamisaye

Culture shock stories from lived experience

According to the experience of students who have been in the UK for over five years, this particular section of the book is dedicated to exploring the real-life experiences and perspectives of individuals who have studied and resided in the United Kingdom. In order to preserve their privacy and confidentiality, the individuals' names will not be disclosed.

Story one

The British are courteous yet incredibly reserved. People in the UK tend not to interact with strangers all that often. I was opportune to live next door to a British man during my first days of arriving in the UK. I always meet this neighbour of mine on my way out of the house and I automatically say, 'Good morning, Sir,' just as my parent had taught me right from childhood. I quote, 'My child, do not ever walk past people without saying hello.' That was the culture I grew up with, and I have done that all my life. But, surprisingly, the British man would not answer my greeting. He tended to repeat this several times of the day each time we met, but the same thing happened. This was rather a shock to me because where I come from, it is a normal thing to say good morning to anyone you meet on your way out of the house, and not acknowledging and responding was rather seen as rude. So I decided to mount up the courage to ask my British neighbour why he always ignores my greeting, and if I have done something wrong. His response shocked me because he had said that he was also very surprised why I always greeted him each time I saw him and felt like I was stalking him. He advised me to please mind my business and not always say good morning or good afternoon or anything like that.

Author's comments: It is important to note that just because someone may have different beliefs or behaviours, it does not necessarily mean that they have no consideration for others. It is crucial to understand and respect individual differences, as this can help create a more accepting and inclusive community. With London's multicultural population, it has been proven through various research and surveys that the city is one of the friendliest in the world. This means that there are numerous opportunities to meet and interact with people from different cultures and backgrounds, which can lead to a greater understanding and appreciation of diversity. By embracing diversity and respecting individual differences, we can create a more harmonious and welcoming environment for everyone.

Story two

If you're prepared to visit the UK, get used to saying and hearing the words "please" and "thank you." Although it may seem like a straightforward gesture, you must always say it. British folks have excellent social skills and are polite and well-mannered. I was on my way to the university one day, and when I got to the bus driver, I simply just said: "Give me a return ticket to the university full stop." The bus driver did not process the ticket, but he gave me a sarcastic look instead. I wondered why he was not responding to what I said, so I repeated the same statement twice again, this time a bit louder because I actually thought he was hard of hearing. The bus driver turned around and said: "Do you have the word please where you come from?" Then the penny dropped. That is when it dawned on me that I was meant to say please at the end of my statement. I was a bit embarrassed because I knew it was polite to say please and thank you, but it did not occur to me that it would be a big deal if I did not say it when I was buying my bus ticket. It was clear that I was not going to get that ticket without saying the magic word. Then I had to this time be a good girl and say, "May I have a return ticket to the university p-l-e-a-se…" Then the bus driver responded, "There you go," and processed my ticket. Ever since then, I have not forgotten my manners. Haha.

Story three

In the United Kingdom, unlike in India, it is generally safe to drink tap water. The government has strict regulations in place to ensure that the water supply is clean and safe. If the water isn't safe to drink, it will be clearly labelled as such. However, while it is safe to drink cold tap water, it's not recommended to use hot water directly from the tap to make hot drinks. Hot water can dissolve lead faster than cold water, meaning that it is more likely to contain higher levels of lead. This is why it is best to either boil the water or use a microwave to heat it up before using it to make hot drinks. It is important to note that water from the hot tap should never be used for drinking, cooking, or making infant formula, as it may contain harmful levels of lead. By taking these precautions, you can ensure that you are consuming clean and safe water.

Story four

International students who come to study in the UK often face various challenges, one of which is language. Even though English is the major language of instruction in many countries, students may still find it difficult to adapt to the language variations and nuances specific to the

UK. In my case, even though I had passed the International English Language Testing System (IELTS) exams with a very high score before coming to England, I was still taken aback by the range of accents that exist in the UK, which were different from what I was used to. As a result, my understanding and speaking of English were impacted. I also realised that my choice of words and phrases varied from the native English speakers in the UK, which made communication more challenging. These language barriers can make it difficult for international students to not only succeed academically but also to integrate socially and emotionally into the UK culture.

How about "flasher"? In British English, a flasher is someone who has a compulsive desire to reveal his genitalia in public. In Nigerian English, it refers to someone who "flashes" or makes a brief call on a cell phone. An acquaintance who had repeatedly "buzzed" my phone on a recent trip to Nigeria joked that she was a "professional flasher"! Before I explained it to her, she had no idea what a "flasher" was or, even worse, what a "professional flasher" meant in British English. Naturally, she was shocked. She enquired if he could use the term "buzzer" since I had previously stated that "buzz" was the word that came closest to capturing the meaning Nigerians intended when they claimed we "flash" someone's phone. However, a buzzer is really another name for a doorbell.

Similarly, the salutation "well done" is particularly Nigerian when used to describe someone who is working. It is used to approximate these expressions by Nigerians: "Sannu chi ma sa" in Mambilla (the author's language), "Sannu da aiki" in Hausa and "Eku ise" in Yoruba, which have no parallels in British English. "Well done" can be used as an adjective in British English to indicate that the meat or food is cooked to a high degree (for example, "I like my food well done"), or as an exclamation that conveys appreciation, similar to the word "bravo." It can also be used as an adjective to characterise work that has been done with expertise and diligence. The practice of saving a particular greeting for those in the workforce is not ingrained in Western culture.

Consider using the word "sorry." Another excellent illustration of linguistic innovation is the way Nigerians utilise the word "sorry." The term's original native English meaning has been stretched from an expression of regret or a simple expression of remorse to one of concern for an unfortunate event (such as someone falling or skipping a step). Whether or not they are to blame for the misfortune, Nigerians use it. This use of the term, which is non-existent in British English, is an approximation of such expressions as "Sannu chi wa" in Mambilla (the author's language) "Sannu fa" in Hausa, "Pele o" in Yoruba, "Ndo" in Igbo, etc. They are all special expressions to express empathy over other people's personal misfortunes. For Nigerians, the British phrases to indicate concern over people's little personal mishaps seem distant and lacking warmth. For example, the British culture would say, "Are you alright?" when someone trips and falls over or something. But a Nigerian would say "Sorry," even if it was not their fault.

Additionally, Nigerians use a plethora of euphemisms that are completely ridiculous in British English, particularly when referring to excretory processes. For example, the phrase "spoil the air" (or its other variants, like "mess", "pollute the air", or just "pollute") is used to refer to fart by Nigerians. The majority of Nigerian cultures are modest and dislike candour when it comes to addressing excretory activities.

Another peculiar Nigerian euphemism that Nigerians use to cover up a lot of sins in the bathroom is "to ease oneself," which I was unaware was specifically Nigerian until I moved to the UK! British natives might say, "I need to go to the toilet," or, if it is a public building, "I need to use the toilet," whereas Nigerians would say, "I want to ease myself" or "I want to piss."

The one that shocked me most was the polite phrase "Spending a penny," which is often used in the UK. Spend a penny means to go to the toilet, especially a public toilet. I used to wonder what penny has to do with going to the toilet. I remember the day I got my first shift to work at a care home, and an elderly man who mobilised with the aid of a wheelchair said to me: "I would like to spend a penny, please." I said to him, "Where is your wallet?" I was asking because I was ready to take him to the shops! Little did I know that he actually wanted me to wheel him to the toilet. Haha! Reflecting on this does make me giggle.

I did my research and found that the expression 'Spend the penny' is derived from the fact that public toilets were installed in the United Kingdom in the mid-1800s that required a penny to be unlocked. Now I know better.

Story five

Another category of language error used by Nigerians is the frequent use of the phrase "barbing salon" to mean hairdressing salon or barber's shop and "barb" to mean receive a haircut. Nigerians use "barb" as a back-formation from barber, which is a hairdresser who cuts hair and shaves beards for a living. However, in British English, "barb" refers to, among other things, the pointy end of a sort of wire. It is also used symbolically to describe an abusive comment made at someone. When used as a verb, it usually implies "provide with barbs," as in "put barbs in a fence." To native English speakers, the use of "barb" to signify "have a haircut" is completely meaningless. So is the expression "barbing salon."

By the way, I do not need to book an appointment to have a haircut in my country. But in the UK, every service you would like to access requires a booked appointment, including hairdressing/a haircut. That was a shock to me. For international students coming to study in the UK, always be prepared to book an appointment before visiting anyone for any kind of service because you may end up wasting your time coming all the way without an appointment. This could include visiting your bank to open a new account, going to your GP if you are unwell, tutorials, etc. You do not just walk in without an appointment except if you have confirmed they do walk-in/drop-in sessions.

There are more stories about Nigerian English because the author happens to be from Nigeria and has spent most of her life with Nigerians. Another example of the use of the English language in Nigeria is the use of the expression "jargon." I used to think that "jargon" meant grammatically faulty, meaningless English. In fact, the term exclusively refers to the specialised technical vocabulary of a group or subject that is normally inaccessible to the general public, such as legal/medical/journalistic jargon. However, it is not uncommon to hear many educated Nigerians accuse others of "speaking jargons" while the accused is speaking clear English. I suppose it is because the phrase sounds similar to "jagajaga," a Nigerian Pidgin English word that encompasses everything Nigerians find offensive. Then there's "colloquial English," which Nigerians use to refer to poor, archaic English. However, in British English, colloquial English merely refers to conversational English, or casual spoken English, as opposed to formal written English. Everyone from the United Kingdom to Nigeria speaks colloquial English in everyday interactions. Perhaps Nigerians dislike the term "colloquial" because it sounds similar to the word "colonial," which has a bad connotation in Nigeria and elsewhere. A lot of international students tend to make this mistake in their essays. The use of colloquial English in academic writing affects the quality of their assignment. It is important to understand the difference between spoken and written English in order to be a successful student in UK universities.

Another Nigerian English term that appears in British English but has a completely different connotation is "go-slow." Nigerians use the phrase "go-slow" to describe a traffic gridlock. In British English, however, "go-slow" is a type of industrial protest in which workers deliberately slow down work in order to achieve demands from their bosses rather than going on strike. Nigerians also use expressions like "he has long legs" instead of "he is well-connected"; "one hell of trouble" instead of "one hell of a lot of trouble"; "you cannot eat your cake and have it" instead of the rather irrational but nevertheless accurate "you cannot have your cake and eat it"; "you can be rest assured that...," instead of "you can rest assured that..."; sweaters instead of jumpers, etc.

Nigerians, for example, define "disvirgin" as "deprive of virginity." However, no word like "disvirgin" can be found in any British English dictionary. Britons use "deflower" to communicate the same meaning as Nigerians do with "disvirgin." Surprisingly, the word "deflower" does not exist in the active idiolect of Nigerians. The word "disvirgin" has even extended the basic definition of "deflower" in contemporary

Nigerian usage. When people use their passports (also known as "international passports" in Nigeria) for the first time, they claim to have "disvirgined" their "international passport!"

Another significant source of this strand of Nigerian English is the conflation of parts of speech. The way Nigerians use the term "opportune" is an example of this type of use error that has gained currency and acceptability. In British English, the word is employed as if it were a verb, but it is actually an adjective. Nigerian politicians frequently use phrases like "I have been opportuned to serve my people" or similar expressions. Opportune, which simply means "well-timed" (for example, "the opportune arrival of the policeman saved him"), cannot have a past tense because it is an adjective rather than a verb.

Perhaps the misunderstanding stems from believing that "opportune" is a derivation of "opportunity." Another common use error in Nigerian

English is the addition of "-ly" to words that are already adverbs. Examples include "outrightly" and "downrightly". These terms are both adjectives and adverbs in British Standard English and do not take the "-ly" form in the sense of "beautifully", "utterly", and so on. The misuse (or, in some cases, lack of use) of prepositions is another area of usage problems from which Nigerian English has developed and continues to emerge.

Nigerians, for example, are fond of asserting that a location is "conducive" without adding the preposition "to" to make a whole sense that is, by British English standards, where "conducive" invariably co-occurs with the preposition "to". Whereas British English speakers say, "Our universities are conducive TO learning," Nigerians respond, "Our universities are conducive."

Other common usage errors that have now become accepted are the use of the term "hot drink" to imply "hard drink", an alcoholic beverage or liquor instead of a cup of tea or coffee; "talk less of" to mean "let alone"; "of recent" to signify "recently" on the model of "of late"; "plate-number" rather than "number-plate"; and "instalmentally" rather than "in instalments". Nigerians also impose the plural form onto words and expressions that don't normally have them in British English. Examples are: "cutleries," "an advice" (instead of "a piece of advice"), " a good news" (instead of simply "good news"), "luggages", "baggages" and "informations" (instead of "bits/pieces of information").

For international students, language can be one of the most daunting challenges to overcome. Even if you have a good command of English, you may still face communication barriers when studying abroad. This is because the way people communicate and express themselves can vary significantly across different cultures. It is important for international students to be aware of these differences and learn how to navigate them in order to fully integrate into their host country and succeed academically. Whether it's understanding colloquial expressions, idioms, or non-verbal communication, being mindful of these nuances can make a significant difference in your ability to connect with others and thrive in your new environment.

www.ingramcontent.com/pod-product-compliance
Lightning Source LLC
Chambersburg PA
CBHW011522070526
44585CB00022B/2503